JOKES TO TICKLE YOUR FUNNY-BONE

Library of Congress Catalog-in-Publication Data
Woodworth, Viki
Jokes to Tickle your Funny bone / Compiled
and illustrated by Viki Woodworth.
p. cm.
Summary: A variety of jokes and riddles
on topics such as food, moms, dads,
and friends.
ISBN 1-56766-207-2
1. Riddles, Juvenile. 2. Wit and humor, Juvenile.
[1. Jokes. 2. Riddles.]
I. Woodworth, Viki.
PN6371.5.J65 1995   95-19547
818.540208--dc20   CIP/AC

JOKES TO TICKLE YOUR FUNNY-BONE

Compiled and Illustrated by
Viki Woodworth

What do you get when you cross a bear with a raincloud?

Drizzly bears.

Evan: What do you get when you cross a bird with a beach?

Karen: Sandy Claws.

What do you get if you cross a penguin and an elephant?

An elephant in a tight tuxedo.

Karen: What do you get when you cross a parrot with a shark?

Evan: A creature that can talk your head off.

What do you get when you cross a parrot with a centipede?

A walkie-talkie.

What do you get when you cross a talkative parrot with a crab?
A gabby crabby.

Why do chimps love bananas?

Because they're so a-peel-ing.

Alex: Why do chimps go to school?

Matt: To learn their Ape-B-C's.

What do you call a helium-filled monkey?

A blimp chimp.

Matt: What do you call a monkey with a sore leg?

Alex: A limp chimp.

What's the smallest monkey?

The shrimpansies.

What kind of monkey do florists like?
Chim-pansies.

What do you call an alligator who prefers to live on the streets?
An alley gator.

Ted: Who always helps the alligator?
Fred: The Gatorade.

What did the crocodile say when he ate the elevator?
"See ya later, elevator."

Fred: Why did the alligator eat the porcupine?
Ted: To floss his teeth.

What kind of fur do you get from a crocodile?
As fur away as possible.

What should you say to a two-headed alligator?
Bye-Bye.

What do you have when an elephant steps on a hippo?

A hippopota-mess.

Barb: What do you call a hippo with a runny nose?

Marg: A drippopotamus.

What do you call it when a hippo has a dirty bathroom?

A hippo-potty-mess.

Marg: Why is a hippo so clumsy?

Barb: It has two left feet.

What do you call an acrobatic hippo?

A flippo-hippo.

What do you call a fast hippo?
A zippo-hippo.

How do snakes tell secrets?

They hissper.

What kind of snake plays the bagpipes?

A piper viper.

Norm: What kind of snake has too much energy?

Deb: A hyper viper.

What kind of snake keeps rain off your windshield?

A windshield viper.

What kind of snake keeps you from having fun?

A boa-restricter.

What kind of snake tells what will happen in the future?
A boa predicter.

Evan: I saw a pig driving down the street.
Dad: Was it a good driver?
Evan: No, it was a road hog!

Baby Owl: Do you think my dad is funny?
Girl Owl: Yes, he's a hoot!

Son Monster: What's for lunch?
Dad Monster: Dread and butter.

Father Squirrel: Where did you put your allowance?
Son Squirrel: In a branch bank.

Father Cow: I just saw Junior fall down in the pasture.
Mother Cow: It's okay. He's on a field trip.

Father Robin: Why are you reading that book?

Daughter Robin: I'm not reading, I'm looking for a bookworm.

What do you get when you cross a hyena with a rhinoceros?

I'm not sure, but if it laughs you'd better laugh too.

Colin: What do you get when you cross a chicken with a ghost?

Aaron: A peck-a-boo.

What do you get when you cross a dog with spaghetti?

Poodle noodles.

Aaron: What do you get when you cross a dog with a tough kid?

Colin: A bully dog.

What do you get if you cross a dog with a piece of fabric?

Mutt-terial.

What do you get when you cross a dog with a hen?
Pooched eggs.

What do you get when you cross a sea creature with a crook?

A monster lobster.

Brittany: What do you get when you cross a barracuda with a Boy Scout?

April: A barracuda who helps old ladies across the ocean.

What do you get when you cross a bore with a seabird?

A dull gull.

April: What do you get when you cross a crocodile with a laughing hyena?

Brittany: A croco-smile.

What do you get when you cross an alligator with germs?

An ill-igator.

What do you get when you cross a sea creature with a strong man?

A mussel-man.

How do eels make ends meet?
They put their tails in their mouths.

Where do fish save their money?
In river banks.

What did the squid say when it ran into the dolphin?
"I didn't do it on porpoise!"

What did the fisherman spread on toast?
Jelly fish.

What kind of fish chases catfish?
Dogfish.

How did the dogfish pay for dinner?
With her credit cod.

What do you get when you cross a hummingbird with a bell?

A humdinger.

Daphne: What do you get when you cross stars with a zebra?

Darron: Stars and Stripes.

What do you get when you cross a dino with a box of toothpicks?

A giant porcupine.

Darron: What do you get when you cross a dino with a parakeet?

Daphne: A messy birdcage.

What do you get when you cross a clown with a skeleton?

Funny bones.

Jason: What do you get when a frog plays baseball?
Dad: I don't know.
Jason: A player who catches flies with his tongue!